MW01093224

". . . The laws of the Lord are true; each one is fair. . . .

They are sweeter than honey, even honey dripping from the comb."

Psalm 19:9-10 NLT

I Love My Bible!

Written and illustrated by
Debby Anderson

CROSSWAY BOOKS • WHEATON, ILLINOIS
A PUBLISHING MINISTRY OF GOOD NEWS PUBLISHERS

"Your word is a lamp to my feet and a light to my path."

Psalm 119:105 ESV

Other Crossway books by Debby Anderson

God Knows My Name, I Can Talk with God, Jesus Is Coming Back

I love My Bible!
Text and illustrations © 2005 by Debby Anderson
Published by Crossway Books
          A Publishing Ministry of Good News Publishers
          1300 Crescent Street, Wheaton, Illinois 60187

Editor: LB Norton. Designer: David LaPlaca.

Scripture references marked NLT are taken from the *Holy Bible, New Living Translation,* copyright © 1996. Used by permission of Tyndale House Publishers, Inc., Wheaton, Ill., 60189. All rights reserved.

Scripture verses marked ESV are taken from *The Holy Bible, English Standard Version.* Copyright © 2001 by Crossway Bibles, a publishing ministry of Good News Publishers. Used by permission. All rights reserved.

Scripture references marked NIV are taken from the *Holy Bible: New International Version*®. Copyright © 1973, 1978, 1984 by International Bible Society. Used by permission of Zondervan Publishing House. All rights reserved. The "NIV" and "New International Version" trademarks are registered in the United States Patent and Trademark Office by International Bible Society. Use of either trademark requires permission of International Bible Society.

Scripture references marked NLV are taken from *New Life Version,* copyright © 1969 by Christian Literature International.

Library of Congress Cataloging-in-Publication Data
Anderson, Debby.
   I love my Bible! / written and illustrated by Debby Anderson.
     p.cm.
   ISBN 1-58134-742-1 (alk. paper)
  1. Bible—Juvenile literature. I. Title.
   BS539.A67 2005
   220—dc22   2005012069

LB	15	14	13	12	11	10	09	08	07	06	05
14	13	12	11	10	9	8	7	6	5	4	3	2	1

To Ronnie Davis,

the answer to our prayers for a loving and

Christ-honoring husband for our daughter, Jenny.

Love, Mom

I love my Bible because it is God's Book! God says that anyone who reads and obeys it will grow strong just like a tree beside a river.

Psalm 1:2-3

We like to read books about dinosaurs
and log cabins and bunnies . . .
but the Bible is the best book in the whole world!

Isaiah 40:7-8

The Bible is different from other books. . . .

It's not just a science book,
even though it tells about animals and floods and the universe.

It's not just a history book,
even though it tells about kings and countries and wars.

It's not a tall tale
like Paul Bunyan . . .

. . . or a fairy tale
like Cinderella . . .

. . . or a made-up
adventure like a
video game.

The Bible is different from other books
because it is God's Word!
It is totally true!

Psalm 119:160

The Bible is also different from other books because it is all about Jesus and how He shows us God's love.

The Bible is full of exciting stories about God's love for people!

John 3:16; 20:31

Ruth

The Stormy Sea

Moses and Miriam

Joseph and His Colorful Coat

The Bible will
never grow old.
It will last forever.

We can read the Bible
our whole life
and still find new things
about God.

Psalm 119:89-90

Even though forty different people wrote parts of the Bible over hundreds of years, it all fits together perfectly. God showed the writers what to say, and they wrote it down in their own special ways.

2 Peter 1:19-21

Except for the Ten Commandments . . .
God wrote those down right into rock!

Paul

Nehemiah

Solomon

David

When you get a new scooter, it comes with instructions that tell the best way to put it together and take care of it.

The Bible is God's instructions for people. Since God is the One who made us, His instructions tell us the best way to live!

2 Timothy 3:16-17

When we memorize God's Word, we have His reminders with us all the time. They're like a light, showing us which way to go.

Psalm 119:105

Writing memory verses on cards helps us to remember them even better!

Eph. 6:1 ESV
Children, obey your parents.

1 Cor. 13:4 ESV
Love is patient.

Psalm 119:11 NLT
I have hidden your word in my heart that I might not sin against you.

God wants everyone to have His Word.
But around the world, many people don't have enough Bibles.
Sometimes they take out pages to give away or
copy pages to share with others.

In some places, they have to keep their Bibles hidden.

Luke 24:45-47

In other places, people do not have a Bible in their language. Missionaries help to put the Bible into other languages.

Let's share and help all people
have Bibles of their own!

Matthew 28:19-20

Bucks
for
Bibles

It's good to read the Bible every day.
You can read it at suppertime . . . at bedtime . . . or anytime!

Psalm 119:147-148

You can read and learn about the Bible at home, at church . . . or anywhere!

Deuteronomy 6:6-9

When we obey and live by God's Word, the Bible says we shine like stars!

Philippians 2:15-16; I John 1:1

"Keep on praying."

1 Thessalonians 5:17 NLT

"Do all things without grumbling..."

Philippians 2:14 ESV

"A cheerful look brings joy..."

Proverbs 15:30 NLT

" ...Be sad with those who are sad."

Romans 12:15 NLV

"Be kind..."

Ephesians 4:32 ESV

" ...Be quick to listen..."

James 1:19 NLT

"...Freely you have received...

...freely give."

Matthew 10:8 NIV

"Thank You, God, for giving us the Bible.
Help us to shine like bright stars by sharing
Your Word and Your love with everyone!"